BRAZIL

Sarah Tieck

VISIT US AT
www.abdopublishing.com

Published by ABDO Publishing Company, PO Box 398166, Minneapolis, MN 55439.

Printed in the United States of America, North Mankato, Minnesota.
092013
092013

 PRINTED ON RECYCLED PAPER

Coordinating Series Editor: Rochelle Baltzer
Contributing Editors: Megan M. Gunderson, Marcia Zappa
Graphic Design: Adam Craven
Cover Photograph: *Glow Images*: © Jim Zuckerman/CORBIS.
Interior Photographs/Illustrations: *AP Photo*: FILIPE ARAUJO/ESTADAO CONTEUDO (Agencia Estado via AP Images) (p. 29), CRIS FAGA/AE/AE (Agencia Estado via AP Images) (p. 15), Robson Fernandjes/Agência Estado/AE (Agencia Estado via AP Images) (p. 29), File (p. 33), DIDA SAMPAIO/ESTADAO CONTEUDO (Agencia Estado via AP Images) (p. 19), Vedada Para Assinantes Brasileiros (p. 33); *Getty Images*: Globo via Getty Images (p. 17), Holger Leue (p. 21), Thomas Marent (p. 23), Prisma/UIG (p. 13), Travelpix Ltd (p. 23); *Glow Images*: Marco Andras (p. 27), Ann Ronan Pictures (p. 31), jspix (p. 23), Yadid Levy (p. 34), SuperStock (p. 25); *iStockphoto*: ©iStockphoto.com/Aquilegia (p. 5), ©iStockphoto.com/josemoraes (p. 9), ©iStockphoto.com/luoman (p. 35), ©iStockphoto.com/ricardoazoury (p. 34); *Shutterstock*: Atlaspix (pp. 19, 38), cifotart (p. 9), Andrej Glucks (p. 37), Luiz Rocha (p. 11), Mark Schwettmann (p. 16), Travel Bug (p. 11), Vitoriano Junior (p. 38), Leanne Vorrias (p. 35).

Country population and area figures taken from the CIA World Factbook.

Library of Congress Control Number: 2013932173

Cataloging-in-Publication Data

Tieck, Sarah.
 Brazil / Sarah Tieck.
  p. cm. -- (Explore the countries)
 ISBN 978-1-61783-805-7 (lib. bdg.)
 1. Brazil--Juvenile literature. I. Title.
 981--dc23
                                                        2013932173

BRAZIL

Contents

Around the World

Our world has many countries. Each country has beautiful land. It has its own rich history. And, the people have their own languages and ways of life.

Brazil is a country in South America. What do you know about Brazil? Let's learn more about this place and its story!

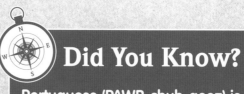
Did You Know?
Portuguese (PAWR-chuh-geez) is the official language of Brazil.

The Amazon rain forest covers the northern part of Brazil. It is the world's largest rain forest.

PASSPORT TO BRAZIL

Brazil is the largest country in South America. It covers about half of the **continent**! Ten countries border it. The Atlantic Ocean forms the eastern border.

Brazil's total area is 3,287,612 square miles (8,514,877 sq km). More than 199 million people live there.

WHERE IN THE WORLD?

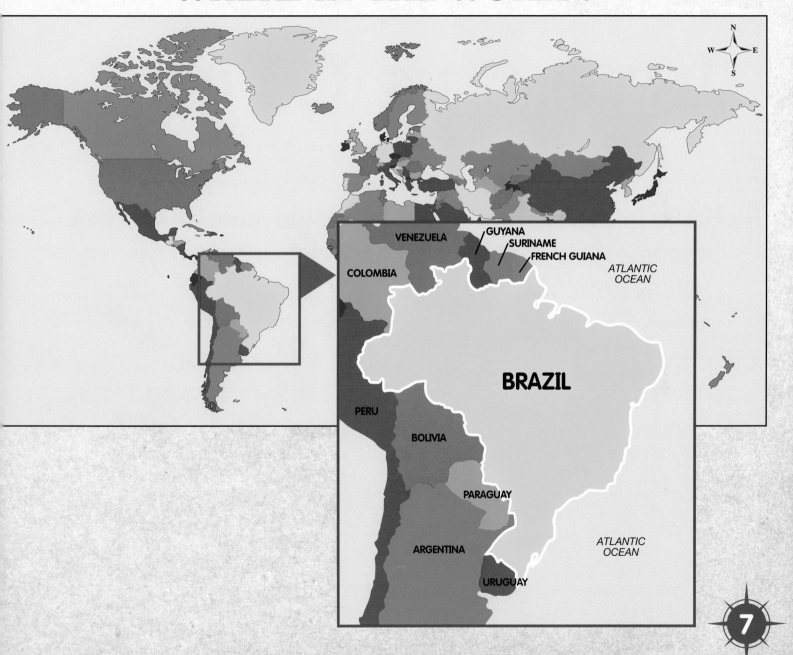

VENEZUELA
GUYANA
SURINAME
FRENCH GUIANA
COLOMBIA
ATLANTIC OCEAN

BRAZIL

PERU

BOLIVIA

PARAGUAY

ARGENTINA

ATLANTIC OCEAN

URUGUAY

Important Cities

Brasília is Brazil's **capital** and fourth-largest city. It is home to more than 2.5 million people. Brasília became Brazil's capital in 1960. It is known for being built from a plan. From above, the city is shaped like a bow and arrow.

São Paulo is Brazil's largest city. It has about 11.3 million people. It was founded in 1554. Today, São Paulo is known for being a center of business.

SAY IT

Brasília
bruh-ZIHL-yuh

São Paulo
SOW POW-loh

BRAZIL

Salvador•

Brasília★

Rio de Janeiro•
São Paulo•

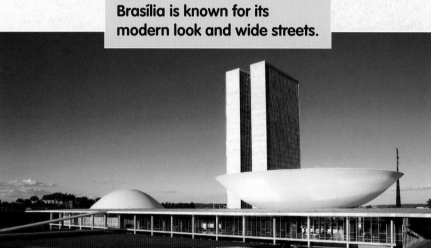

Brasília is known for its modern look and wide streets.

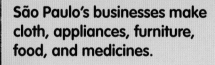

São Paulo's businesses make cloth, appliances, furniture, food, and medicines.

Rio de Janeiro is Brazil's second-largest city. More than 6.3 million people live there. Rio has one of South America's main ports. The city is located between mountains and the ocean. It is a center of business and finance. It is also known for the arts.

Salvador is Brazil's third-largest city, with nearly 2.7 million people. It is a port on Todos os Santos Bay. The city's history dates back to 1549, when it was a Portuguese colony. People visit Salvador to spend time on its white sand beaches.

SAY IT

Rio de Janeiro
REE-oh day zhuh-NEHR-oh

Salvador
SAL-vuh-dawr

Rio de Janeiro is famous for its beaches. It is located on the Atlantic Ocean and Guanabara Bay.

Salvador was built on a steep cliff. People use elevators to go between upper and lower parts of the city.

 Did You Know?

Salvador was Brazil's capital from 1549 to 1763. Rio de Janeiro was the capital from 1763 to 1960.

Brazil in History

The first people to live in Brazil were American Indians. Most formed groups and lived in villages. They hunted and fished. They found food in the forests and grew cassava to eat.

In 1500, the Portuguese claimed the land. In the 1530s, they began to settle it. Brazil became known for its large sugarcane and tobacco farms. Slaves worked on the farms.

In the 1690s and 1700s, diamonds and gold were discovered. People began to move to southeastern Brazil in search of riches.

Pedro Álvares Cabral was a Portuguese explorer. Many say he was the first European to discover Brazil.

13

In 1822, Brazil became independent from Portugal. The years that followed brought many changes. In 1888, slavery became illegal. This freed about 700,000 people. In 1889, Brazil became a **republic**.

As times changed, there was much fighting to control the government. Today, many poor people live in cities and **rural** areas. Also, there is crime. But, Brazil is working to help its people and grow as a country.

Brazil honors Independence Day on September 7.

15

Timeline

1500

Pedro Álvares Cabral landed on the coast of Brazil. He took control of the land for Portugal.

1822

Pedro I became Brazil's first **emperor**. He was forced to step down in 1831. His son Pedro II later ruled the country.

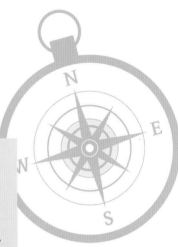

1931

The Christ the Redeemer statue was completed on Mount Corcovado. It looks out over Rio de Janeiro. At 125 feet (38 m) tall, it is one of the world's most famous statues!

1964

"The Girl from Ipanema" by Brazilian songwriters Antônio Carlos Jobim (*left*) and Vinícius de Moraes (*right*) became a worldwide hit! It is a bossa nova song, which is a popular Brazilian music style.

2011

Dilma Rousseff became Brazil's first woman president.

2009

Rio de Janeiro was chosen to host the 2016 Summer Olympics. It was the first South American city chosen to host the games.

An Important Symbol

Brazil's flag was created in 1889. It is green, with a yellow diamond and blue circle in its center. White stars on the blue circle stand for Brazil's states and **capital**. Green and yellow stand for fruitful land and minerals. Blue and white are connected with Portugal's history.

Brazil's government is a **federal republic**. There are 26 states plus the country's capital. Brazil's National Congress makes laws. The president is the head of state and government.

When Dilma Rousseff became president, she wanted to improve women's lives in Brazil. She also wanted health care to be available to more people.

The Portuguese words on Brazil's flag mean "order and progress."

ACROSS THE LAND

Brazil has mountains, coasts, and rain forests. Most of the country is in the **tropics**. This makes it good for growing crops. Brazil's rain forests have many animals, plants, and other **resources**. Its beaches are world famous.

Water is important to Brazil's land. The country borders the Atlantic Ocean. More than 1,000 rivers flow through Brazil! The Amazon River is the largest. The Paraná and São Francisco are also major rivers.

The Amazon River is the world's second-longest river. It begins in Peru and stretches about 4,000 miles (6,400 km). It flows into the Atlantic Ocean.

Did You Know?

In most parts of Brazil, it is warm all year. In July, the average São Paulo temperature is 73°F (23°C).

Many types of animals make their homes in Brazil. Thousands are found in the Amazon rain forest. These include anacondas, boas, monkeys, and toucans. Piranhas, river dolphins, and caimans live in and around rivers.

Brazil's land is home to thousands of different plants. These include Brazil nut and palm trees. Flowers such as orchids grow there. There are even plants that eat bugs, like the pitcher plant!

Green anacondas are among the world's largest snakes. They can be more than 30 feet (9 m) long!

Capybaras are the world's largest rodents. They live in the Amazon rain forest. They can weigh more than 100 pounds (45 kg)!

The Amazon rain forest has a wider variety of plants than any other place on Earth.

Earning a Living

Brazil produces more valuable goods and services than any other South American country. Many people work in factories. They make cars, sugar, steel, shoes, food, and paper. Others have jobs with the government or in schools.

Brazil has many natural **resources**. Amethysts, iron ore, and tin are mined there. Farmers produce coffee beans, sugarcane, and oranges. They raise cattle, chickens, and hogs.

Brazil is the world's leading producer of coffee beans.

LIFE IN BRAZIL

Brazilians live in cities and **rural** areas. Big cities are modern, with tall buildings, museums, and libraries. But they also have **slums**. In rural areas, people live more simply. In the Amazon area, some live in homes with roofs made of leaves.

Traditional Brazilian foods include bananas, coconuts, seafood, beans, cassava, and rice. Fruity drinks, coffee, and mate, which is like tea, are also popular.

Did You Know?

In Brazil, children must attend school from ages 7 to 17. But, this doesn't always happen. Many children are poor and work instead of finishing school. Or, they live in rural areas with no schools.

Feijoada is Brazil's national dish. It includes black beans, pork, and dried beef.

Brazilians enjoy soccer. There, it is called *futebol*. People also enjoy car racing, horse racing, volleyball, and basketball. They spend time on the beaches, too. Favorite activities are swimming, diving, boating, and fishing.

Religion is important in Brazil. Most people belong to the Roman Catholic Church. Many of the country's holidays are connected to this faith.

During Christmastime, a giant Christmas tree stands in São Paulo's Ibirapuera Park.

Brazil has won soccer's World Cup five times. That is more than any other nation!

Did You Know?

Brazilians built new soccer stadiums in order to host the 2014 World Cup!

FAMOUS FACES

Many talented people are from Brazil. Alberto Santos-Dumont was a famous pilot and inventor. He was born on July 20, 1873, in southeast Brazil. In Brazil, he became known as the "Father of Aviation."

Santos-Dumont designed and flew balloons and other types of aircraft. In 1906, he made the first public, powered flight in Europe. He died in 1932.

Santos-Dumont famously flew around the Eiffel Tower in Paris, France, in 1901.

Brazil is known for sports. Pelé is a famous soccer player. He was born on October 23, 1940, in Três Corações. His given name was Edson Arantes do Nascimento.

Pelé started his soccer **career** in 1956. He became famous around the world for his skill. Pelé played 1,363 matches during his career. And, he set a record by scoring 1,281 goals!

Did You Know?

Pelé's father, Joao Ramos do Nascimento, was also a soccer player.

In 1970, Pelé helped the Brazilian national soccer team win its third World Cup!

In 1969, Pelé scored his 1,000th career goal. People gathered at Maracanã Stadium in Rio to cheer for him.

Tour Book

Have you ever been to Brazil? If you visit the country, here are some places to go and things to do!

## Hike

Spend some time in the Amazon rain forest! You'll see thousands of plants, animals, and bugs.

Dance

Celebrate Carnival at the Sambadrome in Rio. This area was designed for parades and street dancing. Some people dance the samba, which started in Brazil. Carnival happens every year before Lent.

 ## Play

Build a sand castle on one of Brazil's white sand beaches. Famous ones include the beaches of Ipanema and Copacabana in Rio.

 ## Explore

Stroll through Ibirapuera Park. It is the largest park in São Paulo. There is a monument to pioneers that built the city.

 ## Cheer

Catch a soccer game in Rio. The city's Maracanã Stadium is one of the world's largest sports stadiums.

A GREAT COUNTRY

The story of Brazil is important to our world. The people and places that make up this country offer something special. They help make the world a more beautiful, interesting place.

Iguaçu Falls is a group of waterfalls on the border between Brazil and Argentina. The famous falls are wider than Niagara Falls!

Brazil Up Close

Official Name: República Federativa do Brasil (Federative Republic of Brazil)

Flag:

Population (rank): 199,321,413 (July 2012 est.) (5th most-populated country)

Total Area (rank): 3,287,612 square miles (5th largest country)

Capital: Brasília

Official Language: Portuguese

Currency: Real

Form of Government: Federal republic

National Anthem: "Hino Nacional Brasileiro" (Brazilian National Anthem)

Important Words

capital a city where government leaders meet.

career work a person does to earn money for living.

continent one of Earth's seven main land areas.

emperor the male ruler of an empire.

federal republic a form of government in which the people choose the leader. The central government and the individual states share power.

republic a government in which the people choose the leader.

resource a supply of something useful or valued.

rural of or relating to open land away from towns and cities.

slum an overcrowded part of a city where poor people live.

tropics areas on Earth that are near the equator where the weather is warm.

Web Sites

To learn more about Brazil, visit ABDO Publishing Company online. Web sites about Brazil are featured on our Book Links page. These links are routinely monitored and updated to provide the most current information available.

www.abdopublishing.com

Index